GREAT TEAMS IN COLLEGE FOOTBALL HISTORY

Luke DeCock

Raintree

Chicago, Illinois

Printed and bound in China by WKT Company Limited

10 09 08 07 06
10 9 8 7 6 5 4 3 2 1

Library of Congress Cataloging-in-Publication Data:

DeCock, Luke.
   Great teams in college football history / Luke DeCock.— 1st ed.
      p. cm. — (Great teams)
   Includes bibliographical references and index.
   ISBN 1-4109-1487-9 (hc) — ISBN 1-4109-1494-1 (pb)
   1. Football teams—United States—History—Juvenile literature. 2.
College sports—United States—History—Juvenile literature. I. Title. II. Series.

GV950.D43 2006
796.332'63'0973—dc22

2005011665

Acknowledgements
The publishers would like to thank the following for permission to reproduce photographs:
College Football Hall of Fame p. 28; Corbis pp. 4 (Underwood & Underwood), 6 (Bettman), 8 (Underwood & Underwood), 11 (Bettman), 24 (Bettman), 31 (Bettman), 12 (Bettman), 18 (Bettman), 17 (Bettman), 27 (Bettman), 35 (Bettman); Empics pp. 10 (AP), 14 (AP), 15 (AP), 21 (AP), 32 (AP/Elise Amendola), 40 (AP/Mike Foley), 42 (AP/Steve Helber); Getty Images pp. 5, 9 (New York Times Co.), 37 (Allsport/Jonathan Daniel), 39 (Allsport/Stephen Dunn), 36 (Stephen Dunn), 33 (Time Life Pictures/Mickey Pfleger); Paul W. Bryant Museum, University of Alabama pp. 20, 23; Reuters p. 41 (Mike Blake); University of Oklahoma, Western History Collections p. 16; Zuma Press pp. 26 (US Presswire), 29 (Sporting News Archives).

Cover image of Jim Crowley in the 1925 Rose Bowl reproduced with permission of Tournament of Roses Archive.

Every effort has been made to contact the copyright holders of any material reproduced in this book. Any omissions will be rectified in subsequent printings if notice is given to the publishers.

The paper used to print this book comes from sustainable resources.

Disclaimer: This book is not authorized or approved by any football team or league.

Contents

Any words appearing in the text in bold, **like this**, are explained in the glossary.

Welcome to the Game

Every year, millions of people look forward to watching the **Super Bowl** and getting a chance to see talented football players competing for a national championship. However, before they become huge superstars in the **National Football League (NFL)**, players learn more about the game of football in college. Playing at the college level is an excellent way for a player to get experience. It is also an important way for them to learn about teamwork. Great college football teams are remembered long after their winning season is over. With determined players, dedicated coaches, and brilliant teamwork the best teams earn a place in sports history!

Columbia University plays against Brown University in a 1920s college football game.

The history of college football goes all the way back to before the 20th century. At first, the sport was mainly played in schools on the East Coast. Eventually, as the game became more popular, it spread all over the United States. Teams in the Midwest, such as the University of Notre Dame Fighting Irish and the University of Michigan Wolverines came to represent the best of college football. After World War II, college football became most popular in the South, and teams in Florida and Texas really stood out. Today, college football has many teams and millions of fans.

Because there is no tournament to determine a national champion, unlike basketball and baseball, every year brings a new **debate** about which college football team is the best. **Bowl games** were created to help decide this. At the end of each college football season, the best teams play in these bowl games. After teams win the bowl games, sportswriters and coaches decide who is the best that year. But usually they don't agree. In fact, there are many arguments each year because it is so hard to pick the best team. Part of the fun of college football is deciding which team you think is the best!

This book picks ten of the greatest college football teams of all time. From the undefeated University of Illinois team in 1923 to the high-scoring 1999 Florida State University Seminoles, this book highlights the coaches and players of the best teams in college football history. A team can be great because of a star **quarterback**, fast **running back**, tough defense, or dedicated coach. However, the greatest teams are often a combination of all of these. After reading this book, you can decide who you think the best teams in college football history are.

1923 University of Illinois Fighting Illini

From his summer job hauling ice in Wheaton, Illinois, Red Grange earned the nickname, "The Wheaton Iceman." From his talented playing on the football field in the fall, he earned the nickname "The Galloping Ghost." Grange wore the number 77 because that was the number he was given at his first University of Illinois practice. It was easy for Grange to score **touchdowns**. Once he broke through a defensive line he was gone, and no one could catch him.

Red Grange leads the Illini team out for another game.

1923 Record

Won	Lost
8	0

Games played

Date	Vs	Result
Oct. 6	Nebraska	W, 24–7
Oct. 13	Butler	W, 21–7
Oct. 20	at Iowa	W, 9–6
Oct. 27	Northwestern (in Chicago)	W, 29–0
Nov. 3	Chicago	W, 7–0
Nov. 10	Wisconsin	W, 10–0
Nov. 17	Mississippi A&M	W, 27–0
Nov. 24	at Ohio State	W, 9–0

W=Win

The first of Grange's three years at Illinois was his best, as well as the team's best. It was 1923 and Grange was on a roll. In his first game, he scored three touchdowns. His 12 touchdowns helped lead the Fighting Illini to a perfect 8–0 season. At the end of the 1923 season, Grange would lead the country in yards gained with 1,260. But the Illini team was made up of more talent than just Grange. For coach Bob Zuppke, it was his third national championship team in ten years. Coach Zuppke's teams were known for great defense, and Grange was able to give the Illini the solid offense they would need to win. Illinois **shut out** its final five opponents, outscoring them 82–0.

HISTORY BOX

College Football Grows

College football was still a young sport in the 1920s. Games drew small crowds and received little attention from the newspapers. In 1923, the Fighting Illini and Red Grange helped change that. Grange was the first college player that fans would pay to see play. Suddenly, schools such as the University of Illinois and the University of Notre Dame built stadiums that could seat 50,000 fans. Grange would go on to make pro football popular when his college days were over. Today, college football games are attended, and watched on television, by millions of fans.

With a perfect 8–0 record, the Illini won the national championship for the first time. Grange's popularity sparked a new interest in college football. After his college career, he would remain in Illinois and play professional football for the Chicago Bears. As Grange did in college, he attracted fans to the games and made professional football more popular than it had been before.

The Illinois team not only won the national championship, but also contributed a lot to the game of college football. Zuppke invented the **huddle** and the **linebacker**, as well as other parts of the game that are used today. Zuppke first used the huddle outdoors in 1921. Before that, it had only been used indoors because the loud cheering of the fans distracted the players. It might be hard to imagine now, but when the huddle was first used, it was not popular and some people even wanted to make it illegal. Today, it is part of every game.

Grange's most famous game came in 1924 against the University of Michigan, a team that had not lost in twenty games. Grange scored six touchdowns that day, the best performance ever in Illinois' Memorial Stadium. He ran the opening kickoff back 95 yards for a touchdown, then scored on a 67-yard run, a 56-yard run, and a 44-yard run. He did this all in the first 12 minutes of the game and Illinois took a 27–0 lead. He added a fifth touchdown and threw for a sixth touchdown later in the game to cement his legend. That day, he totaled 21 carries for 402 yards, and threw 6 passes for 64 yards. It was after this unbelievable game that many newspaper writers started calling Grange the "Galloping Ghost." It seemed like he was invisible to opposing defenses.

Fighting Illini players come together in a huddle.

Grange was such a **dominant** player that he was named part of the **backfield** on Illinois' first All-Century Team, which was a great honor. Some people believe that he is the best running back in college football history. However, Grange was not only great at being a running back. In 1925, after being named an **All-American** running back two years in a row, Grange switched to quarterback, and was named All-American at that position, too! He had so many moves and with his quickness, agility, and ability to dodge tacklers, he was almost impossible to bring down. Zuppke knew how unstoppable Grange was and so he handed the ball off to him about 30 times every game. Grange scored 31 touchdowns for the University

Harold "Red" Grange (1903–1991)

Red Grange was football's first star, for both college and pro. At Illinois, he dominated the country for three years. If there had been a **Heisman Trophy** back then, Grange might have won it three times. No player in the country was as fast as Grange, and no player could score as many touchdowns. Grange helped make pro football popular, too. After the 1925 season, Grange went on a 67-day coast-to-coast tour to **promote** the new league. Grange was so popular he drew huge crowds everywhere he went.

1924 University of Notre Dame Fighting Irish

At a time when college football was most popular on the East Coast, coach Knute Rockne's success at the University of Notre Dame helped spread the game to the Midwest. Coaching for the Fighting Irish, Rockne had three national titles and five undefeated teams. Who knows what Rockne and Notre Dame would have accomplished had he not died tragically in a plane crash in 1931 at age 43.

College football was just becoming popular in the 1920s when sportswriter Grantland Rice called Notre Dame's 1924 backfield "The Four Horsemen." The team was unbeaten that year. Quarterback Harry Stuhldreher, **fullback** Elmer Layden, and **halfbacks** Jimmy Crowley and Don Miller were four of the best players in the country. In 1921, Stuhldreher impressed Coach Rockne.

The 1924 Notre Dame offense lines up.

All-Americans

Harry Stuhldreher (QB)
Jimmy Crowley (HB)
Elmer Layden (FB)
Bud Boeringer (C)

QB=Quarterback,
FB=Fullback, C=Center

In the next three years, Stuhldreher would become a great quarterback who was able to read defenses and call out the plays that led to touchdowns. Weighing only 154 pounds, Stuhldreher was small for a college football player. In fact, he was the smallest of the "Four Horsemen." Stuhldreher didn't let his size stop him. He was fast and dodged the opposing defensive players with quick moves. Despite his size, Stuhldreher did not get hurt very often and he was never afraid to carry the football against bigger, stronger players. He was named to the All-American team after the 1924 season.

"The Four Horsemen" of Notre Dame pose for a picture in 1924.

HISTORY BOX

An Unmatched Tradition

Considered to be the first college-football powerhouse, the University of Notre Dame built a tradition in the 1920s under coach Knute Rockne that still lives on today. Today, with movies such as *Rudy* showing the level of fame the Fighting Irish have achieved, Notre Dame continues to be a huge name in college football. True to its fans, Notre Dame was one of the first schools to build a stadium that could hold more than 20,000 fans and has kept it filled for decades.

Jimmy Crowley was nicknamed "Sleepy Jim" because he always looked tired. He had slumped shoulders, a slow walk, and always seemed to be relaxed. Crowley was not the fastest player on the field, but he used good moves to get by the players defending him. He would wait until they came at him, and then fake one way while the defender went the other. Crowley, like Stuhldreher, was small at 158 pounds. Also like Stuhldreher, he did not let his size get the best of him. Crowley was fearless and ran into the defense as hard as he could. During his career, he ran the ball for a total of 1,932 yards. He was also an All-American.

Knute Rockne (1888–1931)

Knute Rockne helped spread the fame of both Notre Dame and college football through his work with the fans and determination on the field. A Notre Dame graduate, he was only 26 years old when he started coaching the Fighting Irish. He was one of the first coaches to use the forward pass as a weapon in offense. Rockne will always be remembered both for his success—his teams went 105–12–5—and his famous speeches. It was Rockne who **inspired** his team to "Win one for the Gipper."

Elmer Layden was one of the fastest players on the Fighting Irish. He weighed 164 pounds and was the biggest of the "Four Horsemen." He played the fullback position because of his larger size. Although Layden had injured his knee in high school, he didn't let the injury stop him. He used his determination and skills to earn a spot on the team. Layden earned All-American honors for the Fighting Irish. He was also a star player on the defense, where he was able to easily **intercept** many of his opponent's passes. Layden was very valuable to Notre Dame because of his ability to play both offensive and defensive positions.

1924 Record

Won	Lost	Rose Bowl
10	0	Beat Stanford University 27–10

Games played

Date	Vs	Result
Oct. 4	Lombard	W, 40–0
Oct. 11	Wabash	W, 34–0
Oct. 18	at Army (in NY)	W, 13–7
Oct. 25	at Princeton	W, 12–0
Nov. 1	Georgia Tech	W, 34–3
Nov. 8	at Wisconsin	W, 38–3
Nov. 15	Nebraska	W, 34–6
Nov. 22	Northwestern	W, 13–6
Nov. 29	at Carnegie Tech	W, 40–19

Rose Bowl, Pasadena, California

Jan. 1	Stanford	W, 27–10

In the 30 games the Four Horsemen played together, they lost only twice. None of them were taller than 6 feet or weighed more than 165 pounds, but they put their talents to use in the game. In 1924, they had their best season. The Four Horsemen ran behind an offensive line the fans called "The Seven Mules." Notre Dame beat the United States Military Academy Army Cadets 13–7 in October and breezed through the rest of their schedule. The Fighting Irish finished their season with a 27–10 victory over Stanford University in the Rose Bowl. This was just the beginning of the University of Notre Dame's college football success. Since then, the Fighting Irish have won ten more national titles.

Earl "Red" Blaik came to the United States Military Academy from Dartmouth in 1941 and recruited some of the nation's best players to the military academy during World War II. He had so much talent that he formed two separate teams in 1944, with each team playing two **quarters**. The Army Cadets dominated opponents and outscored them 504–35 in 9 games. However, as impressive as the 1944 team was, Army was even better in 1945.

Army's national championship team in 1945 was built around a pair of running backs who became known as "Mr. Inside" and "Mr. Outside." Mr. Outside, Glenn Davis, would run to the edges of the field, speeding past the defense. Davis followed the blocks of his teammates, especially Felix "Doc" Blanchard, to gain yards on runs. During the 1944 season, Davis scored 20 touchdowns for Army, many of them coming on very long runs. In his college career, he scored a total of 59 touchdowns! He was also named to the All-American team for three straight years in 1944, 1945, and 1946! Davis won the Heisman Trophy in 1946, which is the greatest award for a player in college football.

"Mr. Inside," Felix Blanchard was also a great player. He would run down the middle of the field because he was big and strong. He struck fear into those who were trying to tackle him. Blanchard's combination of quickness and physical strength made him unstoppable.

Army player Felix Blanchard (#35) avoids being tackled by Michigan players.

Not only were defenders scared when he had the ball, but they were also scared when Blanchard was running at them to block them. He was a dedicated player who stopped at nothing to get the job done. Blanchard was also the **punter** for Army, with kicks so high the opposing team had trouble returning the ball. He could punt the ball 50 or 60 yards, giving his team a field advantage. He was named to the All-American team three times and was one of the most flexible players in college football history.

The University of Chicago's Jay Berwanger was the first player to receive the Heisman Trophy.

Few teams had the talent during the War to defend against both Davis and Blanchard. Blanchard won the Heisman Trophy in 1945 as a junior, while Davis beat him for it in 1946 as a senior. Blanchard scored 19 touchdowns in 1945. Davis had 20 touchdowns in 1944 to lead the nation. In their 3 seasons together, the United States Military Army Cadets went 27–0–1.

1945 Record

Won	Lost
9	0

Games played

Date	Vs	Result
Sept. 29	Louisville Army Air Field	W, 32–0
Oct. 6	Wake Forest	W, 54–0
Oct. 13	Michigan	W, 28–7
Oct. 20	Melville Navy Base	W, 55–13
Oct. 27	Duke	W, 48–13
Nov. 3	Villanova	W, 54–0
Nov. 10	Notre Dame	W, 48–0
Nov. 17	at Pennsylvania	W, 61–0
Dec. 1	Navy	W, 32–13

All-Americans

Glenn Davis (HB)
Felix Blanchard (FB)
Tex Coulter (T)
Hank Foldberg (E)
John Green (G)
Albert Nemetz (T)

T=Tackle, E=End

1956 University of Oklahoma Sooners

Just when Notre Dame was setting a new standard for great college football, the University of Oklahoma was creating a great team of its own. The key to this team was a coach named Bud Wilkinson. He had played for Minnesota before World War II. Wilkinson came to Oklahoma as a young, 31-year-old coach in 1947. Oklahoma wasn't known as a football state, and Wilkinson wanted to change that.

The 1956 University of Oklahoma Sooners pose for a photo.

Wilkinson was so successful that by the time he left in 1963, the Sooners had won 3 national titles and 47 games in a row from 1953 to 1957—a Division I record that may never be broken. Wilkinson got off to a good start by winning a national title in his fourth season in 1950. His teams of the mid-1950s would make him a great coach. Oklahoma's winning streak began in the third game of the 1953 season and lasted until 1957. The Sooners would go on to lead the nation in nearly every offensive category in 1955 and 1956, winning the national title in both seasons.

All-Americans

Tommy McDonald (HB)
Ed Gray (T)
Bill Krisher (G)
Jerry Tubbs (C)

Bud Wilkinson (1916–1994)

Bud Wilkinson grew up in Minnesota and played for the Minnesota Golden Gophers, so he knew about playing for a hometown team. That's how he built his program at Oklahoma. Wilkinson recruited players from within 150 miles of the school's campus in Norman, Oklahoma. Organized and prepared, Wilkinson was into the details of the game, and his attitude helped his team win. In 1956, he recruited Oklahoma's first African-American player, Prentice Gautt. Wilkinson's teams won thirteen **conference** titles in a row, and the Oklahoma Sooners became one of the country's best football teams.

Bud Wilkinson prepares his team for a game in 1956.

The 1956 Sooners defeated Texas 45–0 and beat the University of Notre Dame 40–0. They scored 466 points in 10 games and shut out 6 of their opponents. The winning streak would go on until the next season and reach a total of 47 games. Oklahoma's 1956 team was very dangerous on both the offense and defense. They were so good at running the ball that they set a record when they averaged just under 400 rushing yards a game.

17

The 1956 championship Orange Bowl game is remembered as one of the best and most exciting games in college football history. Both Oklahoma and the University of Maryland Terrapins entered the game undefeated. The Sooners were on a 29-game winning streak, and the Terrapins were on a 15-game winning streak. Maryland had one of the best defenses in college football and Oklahoma had a record-setting running game. Fans were excited to see which side would come out victorious.

Maryland started stronger than the Sooners and had them down 6–0 at the halftime of the 1956 Orange Bowl. Many people thought that the Sooner's long winning streak was going to come to an end. In the locker room, Coach Wilkinson shouted at his players, telling them they would lose badly unless they started to play like they had been playing all season. The players were shocked that Wilkinson was so angry, but they were determined to play better. The shouting paid off. The Sooners scored twenty points to cap their national title season.

Tommy McDon was named t the All-Americ team in 1956

Bowling for Titles

Major bowl games were played after the season for years, but it wasn't until the 1950s that they became what they are today. After Oklahoma sealed its national title with an Orange Bowl victory in 1956, **National Collegiate Athletic Association (NCAA)** rules stopped them from returning to a bowl game the next season. But bowl games were good for television, and their popularity forced a change in the rules. Today, bowl games are a way for teams to show how good they are and to help decide the national title. They are also a way for the universities and colleges with football teams to raise money.

The turning point for the Sooners came when Tommy McDonald returned a punt for 32 yards, and then scored on a four-yard run on the next play, giving his team their first lead of the game. On their next possession, the Sooners drove the ball down field and scored on a quarterback **sneak**. After that, a fourth quarter interception by cornerback Carl Dodd sealed the game. He returned it 82 yards for a touchdown. Sooners' quarterback Jim Harris also played a great game, instructing his team and giving them orders in the huddle so quickly that the Maryland defense could not keep up.

1956 Record

Won	Lost	Rose Bowl
11	0	Beat Maryland 20–6

Games played

Date	Vs	Result
Sept. 29	North Carolina	W, 36–0
Oct. 6	Kansas State	W, 66–0
Oct. 13	at Texas	W, 45–0
Oct. 20	at Kansas	W, 34–12
Oct. 27	at Notre Dame	W, 40–0
Nov. 3	at Colorado	W, 27–19
Nov. 10	at Iowa State	W, 44–0
Nov. 17	Missouri	W, 67–14
Nov. 24	Nebraska	W, 54–6
Dec. 1	at Oklahoma State	W, 53–0

The 1956 Sooners were so talented that they had two different players on the All-American team—center Jerry Tubbs and halfback Tommy McDonald. They also had kicker Clendon Thomas who led the entire country in scoring, with 108 points. The team was number one in the entire country in scoring, rushing yards, and total offensive yardage.

1961 University of
Alabama Crimson Tide

For 25 years, Paul "Bear" Bryant coached on the sidelines at the University of Alabama, often wearing a checkered hat on his head. Bryant was a firm believer in rules and order, and his teams were tough both mentally and physically. In the 1960s and 1970s, Bryant put together teams at Alabama that other teams in the college football world would grow to respect for years.

The 1961 Alabama team.

Bryant made his mark as a coach at Texas A&M University, where he took his first team to the remote town of Junction, Texas, in 1954. In 10 days of brutal workouts in hot weather, 76 players quit. Two years later, Texas A&M had an unbeaten season. The University of Alabama brought in Bryant in 1958 to help their struggling football program. Bryant had actually played for Alabama's team when he was a college student. In 1935, he helped Alabama to a 10–0 record and a Rose Bowl appearance. Right away he promised to win a national title. Four years later, the Crimson Tide won its first national title in twenty years, thanks entirely to players that Bryant had brought into the program. This was Bryant's first of 6 titles in 25 years at Alabama. When he was a coach, he held the record for the most wins by a coach in college football history, with 323 wins, 85 losses, and 7 ties.

Some consider Bryant to be one of the greatest coaches in college football history. He had 37 winning seasons. During the 1960s and 1970s no school in the entire nation had a better winning record than Bryant's Alabama teams. Bryant had the ability to make his players better than they ever thought they could be, and to make them perform well together as a team. Bryant's teams were respected and well known for their ability to be tough and play great football. He actually demanded that every player be the best he could be. Back as a college football player, Bryant had played in a game against Tennessee with a broken leg! So he expected nothing less than the best from his players.

Paul Bryant is one of the most successful coaches in college football history.

Paul "Bear" Bryant (1913–1983)

Growing up on a farm in Alabama, Paul Bryant was one of twelve children. He played football at Alabama and became an assistant coach there after graduating in 1936. After World War II, he was hired as head coach at Maryland and then Kentucky before taking over at Texas A&M. Bryant returned to Alabama in 1958 and won 6 national titles in 25 years. His strict discipline kept the Crimson Tide successful. He retired after the 1982 season as the all-time leader in coaching wins with 323; a record that stood strong for 20 years. Bryant died less than a month after coaching his last game.

Quarterback Pat Trammell and **lineman** Billy Neighbors were the big stars for Alabama in 1961. Neighbors was even named to the All-American team. Linebacker Lee Roy Jordan was the Crimson Tide's biggest defensive star and he stopped any opposing player from coming in his path. Alabama outscored its opponents 297–25. Alabama didn't allow the other team to score a point in the last five games of the regular season. Their defense was almost impossible to score against, just as Bryant had wanted it to be. All of the team's hard practices had paid off.

In the Sugar Bowl, the Crimson Tide jumped out to a 10-point lead in the first half. Quarterback Pat Trammell scored the touchdown, and kicker Tim Davis scored the **extra point** and **field goal**. Alabama did not score again and held on to win 10–3 over the University of Arkansas for the national title. Because of their huge season, the Crimson Tide won Coach Bryant the Coach of the Year Award. In 1961, Alabama had won all of their games for the first time since 1945. The 1961 title was just the beginning for Alabama. The Crimson Tide won the national championship again in 1964 and 1965, and then three more times in 1973, 1978, and 1979.

All-Americans

Billy Neighbors (T)

1961 Record

Won	Lost	Sugar Bowl
11	0	Beat University of Arkansas 10–3

Games played

Date	Vs	Result
Sept. 23	at Georgia	W, 32–6
Sept. 30	Tulane	W, 9–0
Oct. 7	at Vanderbilt	W, 35–6
Oct. 14	N.C. State	W, 26–7
Oct. 21	Tennessee	W, 34–3
Oct. 28	at Houston	W, 17–0
Nov. 4	Mississippi State	W, 24–0
Nov. 11	Richmond	W, 66–0
Nov. 18	Georgia Tech	W, 10–0
Dec. 2	Auburn	W, 34–0

Sugar Bowl, New Orleans

Jan. 1	Arkansas	W, 10–3

Split Down the Middle

With no national championship game, the only way to determine a national champion in football during the second half of the 20th century was through the **polls**. Since 1950, there have been 2 major polls—The Associated Press (AP) poll of sportswriters and the UPI or ESPN/*USA Today* poll of football coaches. These polls haven't always agreed because before 1974 the coaches voted before the bowl games were even played. In 1973, Alabama was UPI's pick, but Notre Dame was first in the AP poll. They could both claim to be national champions. Even today, there are still problems. After split titles in 1990, 1991, and 1997, the **Bowl Championship Series (BCS)** was formed in 1998 to match the top two teams in a title game, but failed to do so in 2003. That year the BCS system for picking the top teams picked a team with two losses to play for the title over a team with one loss.

Lee Roy Jordan was a crucial part of Crimson Tide's incredible defense.

1971 University of Nebraska Cornhuskers

On Thanksgiving Day in 1971, top-ranked Nebraska and second-ranked University of Oklahoma met in what was called "The Game of the Century." The defending national champion Nebraska traveled to Norman, Oklahoma, for the game. Since both teams were undefeated, the game was sure to be a tough one. Nebraska had the nation's top-ranked defense, while Oklahoma had the nation's top-ranked offense.

Nebraska's Jeff Kinney flies after getting tripped in a game against Oklahoma on November 25, 1971.

Nebraska's Johnny Rodgers ran a punt back 72 yards for a touchdown in the first quarter to give the Cornhuskers an early lead. But it was a back-and-forth game that came down to Nebraska's final drive in the fourth quarter. The Cornhuskers scored with a little over a minute and a half to play for a 35–31 win. Another Cornhusker who played a great game was middle guard Rich Glover, who finished the game with an amazing 22 tackles. Glover had a huge play at the end of the game, where he deflected a fourth-down Sooners' pass with under a minute remaining in the game and ended the chances for an Oklahoma comeback.

All-Americans

Johnny Rodgers (RB)
Rich Glover (MG also known as an NG)
Willie Harper (DE)
Larry Jacobson (DT)

RB=Running Back, MG=Middle Guard, NG=Nose Guard, DE=Defensive End, DT=Defensive Tackle

1971 Record

Won	Lost	Orange Bowl
13	0	Beat University of Alabama 38–6

Games played

Date	Vs	Result
Sept. 11	Oregon	W, 34–7
Sept. 18	Minnesota	W, 35–7
Sept. 25	Texas A&M	W, 34–7
Oct. 2	Utah State	W, 42–6
Oct. 9	at Missouri	W, 36–0
Oct. 16	Kansas	W, 55–0
Oct. 22	at Oklahoma State	W, 41–13
Oct. 30	Colorado	W, 31–7
Nov. 6	Iowa State	W, 37–0
Nov. 13	at Kansas State	W, 44–17
Nov. 25	at Oklahoma	W, 35–31
Dec. 4	at Hawaii	W, 45–3

Orange Bowl, Miami

Jan. 1	Alabama	W, 38–6

The game was as close as any team would come to beating Nebraska that season. Oklahoma was the only team to lead the Cornhuskers at any time. Third-ranked Colorado lost 31–7. Even a powerful, undefeated Alabama team couldn't come close; losing to Nebraska 38–6 in the Orange Bowl. In that game, the Cornhuskers took a 28–0 halftime lead thanks to a Rodgers punt return and three rushing touchdowns.

The Cornhuskers averaged a record 437 yards on offense while scoring 39.1 points per game, which was good for third in the country. Nebraska only allowed 8.2 points per game. It was their defense that made them unbeatable. They were ranked second in the country in rushing yards allowed, third in points allowed, and fifth in total defense. At one point, the Cornhuskers went twelve straight quarters without allowing a point. During that time, they had two shutouts against conference opponents. They defeated University of Missouri 36–0 and University of Kansas 55–0.

Rich Glover went on to win two major defensive player awards the next season. Glover also was named twice to the All-American team along with tackle Larry Jacobson, end Willie Harper, and John Dutton.

The 1971 Cornhuskers had both a strong defense and offense.

HISTORY BOX

Equipped for Safety

Today, football players wear plenty of safety equipment such as helmets, shoulder pads, and kneepads. This wasn't always the case. In the early days, players wore only soft leather helmets. In the 1950s, players started wearing hard plastic helmets like the ones used today. Facemasks were also added in the 1950s. Nebraska's 1971 national championship team was one of the last teams not to use mouthpieces. By 1973, every player needed a mouthpiece to protect his teeth.

Johnny Rodgers (1951–   )

Most of the time, the Heisman Trophy goes to a great running back or quarterback. Johnny Rodgers (#20, pictured below) was neither. He could play almost any position, although he was at his best returning kicks and punts. Nebraska was a team that liked to run the ball, so the Cornhuskers didn't throw the ball to him often. But when they did, Rodgers was fast and very hard to tackle. Even though he didn't have the statistics of other players, he won the Heisman Trophy in 1972 because he could score almost every time he got the ball.

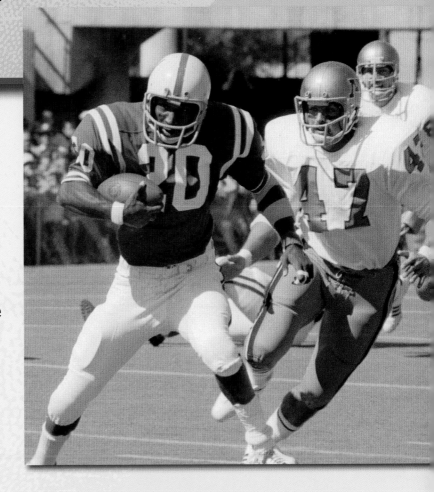

With four players on the defensive side all named to the All-American team during their careers it shows just how great the 1971 Cornhuskers' defense was. Not only was the defense very hard to get through, they were also able to intercept passes and force turnovers very easily. They set a school record for turnovers caused, by recovering 20 fumbles and intercepting 27 passes!

Quarterback Jerry Tagge and receiver Johnny Rodgers led the offense. Rodgers was also a terrific punt and kick returner. He always gained a lot of yards when he received the ball. Because of the great field position that he set up for the offense, they were able to score easily against opponents. Their Orange Bowl win to finish the season ran Nebraska's winning streak to 23 games. That streak ended the next season, but that year Rodgers won the Heisman Trophy. The 1971 Cornhuskers were truly a powerful team.

For almost two decades, and under two different coaches, the University of Southern California had many powerful 1,000-yard tailbacks and Heisman Trophy winners. The Trojans won four national titles on the strength of a running game built around great runners such as O.J. Simpson, Anthony Davis, Ricky Bell, and Charles White. USC was always known for having great running backs, and even though opposing teams knew this, it was still very hard to stop them.

With sophomore Davis handling the running in 1972, USC had a team that was unstoppable. Receiver Lynn Swann and **tight end** Charles Young caught passes from quarterbacks Mike Rae and Pat Haden, while Davis ran for the first of his three seasons. Davis was thirteenth in voting for the Heisman Trophy Award in 1973, and second in voting in 1974. He was also voted as an All-American in 1974.

The 1972 University of Southern California Trojans pose for a photo.

Lynn Swann (1952-   )

Even though he was a great wide receiver, Lynn Swann had to work very hard at football. As a boy, his mom made him take ballet lessons. Those lessons paid off when he could dodge tacklers like a dancer. Swann was small, but he was fast and could avoid defenders instead of knocking them over. At Southern California, he played on the great 1972 team and was an All-American in 1973. In the NFL, he won the Super Bowl with the Pittsburgh Steelers. After he retired, Swann became a television sports broadcaster.

Lynn Swann was a great receiver. In 1973, he was named as an All-American and finished twelfth in the voting for the Heisman Trophy Award. During his career at Southern California, Swann caught 85 passes and averaged 17 yards per catch. Swan was very fast and could jump very well. Because of this, he was able to beat his defenders down the field and make great leaping catches.

All-Americans

Pete Adams (T)
Booker Brown (T)
Sam Cunningham (RB)
Anthony Davis (RB)
John Grant (DT)
Artimus Parker (DB)
Lynn Swann (WR)
Richard Wood (LB)
Charles Young (TE)

WR=Wide Receiver,
LB=Linebacker, TE=Tight End

Linebacker Richard Wood was an All-American, and made the team's defense very tough to get through. The Trojans' defense was so good that they never gave up a run longer than 29 yards! They also intercepted an amazing 28 passes from opponents. USC outscored opponents 467–134, and never trailed in the second half of a single game, going 12–0 and winning the national title for coach John McKay in the Rose Bowl.

McKay was one of the great coaches in college football history. He earned coach of the year in 1962 and 1972. He won a total of four national championships in his career, all at USC. He was determined that his team should play their best, and the Rose Bowl wasn't just a game for him. In the Rose Bowl, USC showed just how good they were when they beat Ohio State University 42–17. All of the players for USC had great games. Running back Sam Cunningham scored 4 touchdowns, while his teammate Anthony Davis ran for 157 yards on 23 carries, including a touchdown run of 20 yards. He also caught 3 passes in the game for 17 yards. Lynn Swann caught 6 passes for 108 yards, including a 10-yard touchdown catch.

HISTORY BOX

Student Body Left, Student Body Right

One of the reasons Southern California built such a great tradition of tailbacks was that USC recruited and developed some of the best offensive linemen in the country. Using plays made popular by the Green Bay Packers in the late 1960s, the Trojans would put their big offensive linemen outside to block and let their tailbacks find the holes in the other team's defense. These plays came to be nicknamed "student body left" and "student body right" because so many players were moving in those directions. It wasn't until defenses became faster and quicker in the 1980s that this type of power running became less popular.

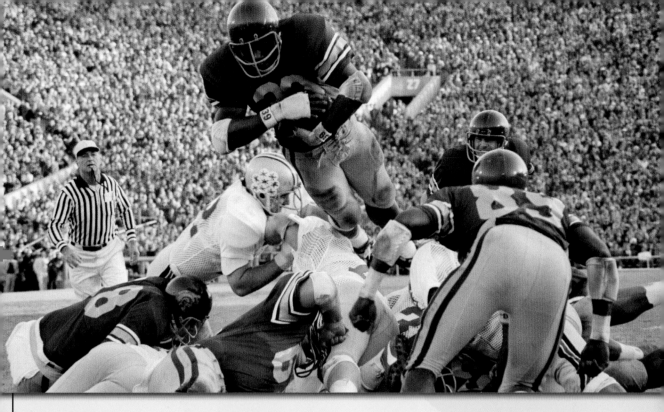

USC's Sam Cunningham dives with the ball in the Rose Bowl. USC won 42–17 over Ohio State.

In 1972, the Trojans beat a total of five ranked teams, making them one of the most dominant college football teams ever. After that, the Trojans became the first team in history to receive every single number one vote on both the coaches and media polls. Davis would also make his mark two years later against Notre Dame. Down 24–0, the Trojans scored 55 points in less than 17 minutes against the number 1 defense in the country. Davis caught a touchdown pass, ran a kickoff back for a touchdown and ran for two more as USC went on to win its second national in three seasons. Charles Phillips, who ran back three interceptions for touchdowns, led USC's aggressive defense.

1972 Record

Won	Lost	Rose Bowl
12	0	Beat Ohio State University 42–17

Games played

Date	Vs	Result
Sept. 9	at Arkansas	W, 31–10
Sept. 16	Oregon State	W, 51–6
Sept. 23	at Illinois	W, 55–20
Sept. 30	Michigan State	W, 51–6
Oct. 7	at Stanford	W, 30–21
Oct. 14	California	W, 42–14
Oct. 21	Washington	W, 34–7
Oct. 28	at Oregon	W, 18–0
Nov. 4	at Washington State	W, 44–3
Nov. 18	at UCLA	W, 24–7
Dec. 2	Notre Dame	W, 45–23

Rose Bowl, Pasadena, California

Jan. 1	Ohio State	W, 42–17

1986 Pennsylvania State University Nittany Lions

After producing many NFL stars, Penn State gained a reputation as the best school for NFL linebackers. In 1986, senior Shane Conlan was next on the list. A hard-hitting inside linebacker, he was one of the hardest-working players in the country. Trey Bauer played next to Conlan. He wasn't as well known, but he was just as effective. Together, they helped bring Penn State a national title.

Penn State's D.J. Dozier (42) leaps past Boston College's Bill Romanowski.

Joe Paterno took over as Penn State's coach in 1966 and began a career that would span five decades. After three undefeated seasons earlier in his career, Paterno finally won a national title in 1982 with a win over the University of Georgia in the Sugar Bowl. Paterno also coached an undefeated team in 1994, but they ended up losing the national championship game. Paterno once coached ten straight teams that made it to bowl games, starting in the 1973 season and stretching all the way to the 1983 season.

The 1986 team was considered to be Paterno's best. It truly represented the spirit of Penn State and Paterno's program. He didn't believe in star players or flashy football playing. Paterno wanted his teams to play together and to work hard on defense. They didn't score a lot of points, but the team didn't give up many either. In 1986, their defense carried them to an undefeated regular season. Paterno was such a great coach that he was named Coach of the Year in 1968, 1978, 1982, and 1986.

Paterno not only cared about his team doing well on the field, he also wanted them to do well in school. He called it his "Grand Experiment" and required that his students do well in the classroom. Because of Paterno's guidance Penn State became known as having great football teams with smart players who would do more than just play football.

Joe Paterno (1926–   )

Eleven different men have been United States President since Joe Paterno became coach at Penn State. He was 23 when he joined Penn State's coaching staff, and 40 when he was named head coach in 1966. He became known as a coach who put education ahead of victory on the football field. Five of his teams were undefeated and two won national titles. Only Amos Alonzo Stagg coached for more years at one school (the University of Chicago) than Paterno has coached at Penn State. Only three coaches have won more games than Paterno. To this day, he refuses to allow players' names on the backs of Penn State's plain white jerseys, because he feels the team is more important than each individual player.

Running back D. J. Dozier led the Penn State offense. He was named an All-American in 1986, and finished eighth in the Heisman Trophy voting. He ran for 811 yards during the season and averaged 4.7 yards per carry, while scoring 10 touchdowns. He also caught two passes for touchdowns. Dozier had played in the 1983 Aloha Bowl and scored the winning touchdown with a 2-yard run, with only 3 minutes to go in the game. Dozier was a tough runner and had a lot of determination, and it showed in his playing.

In the Fiesta Bowl, Penn State played the University of Miami Hurricanes for the national title. These two teams couldn't have been more different. The Hurricanes were loud and arrogant and wore military uniforms around Phoenix during the week of the bowl game to show how tough they were. With Miami quarterback Vinny Testaverde tossing the football to plenty of All-Americans, the Hurricanes were very confident.

However, Penn State's defense was too good for Miami. Running back D.J. Dozier helped Penn State keep the ball out of Miami's hands. He had a great game, rushing for 99 yards on 20 carries.

All-Americans

Shane Conlan (LB)
Chris Conlin (OT)
D.J. Dozier (HB)
Tim Johnson (DT)

OT=Offensive Tackle

HISTORY BOX

Bowls Get Bigger

When Penn State and Miami played in the 1987 Fiesta Bowl, each team received $2.4 million. In 2003, when Miami and Ohio State played for the national title in the Fiesta Bowl, each team received $14.3 million. That's a lot more than the $168,237 Florida State and Arizona State received for playing in the first Fiesta Bowl back in December 1971. Because so much money is involved in bowl games, college football doesn't have a national tournament to determine a champion like the one in college basketball.

Dozier scored the winning touchdown with just over 8 minutes to play on an 8-yard run. Because of the great game that Dozier had, he was named the game's Most Outstanding Offensive Player. Behind Dozier, Penn State gave the Hurricanes' defense problems. When the Hurricanes had the ball, Penn State's defense took it away. The Nittany Lions intercepted Testaverde 5 times for a 14–10 victory. Conlan had two of those interceptions to cap off a remarkable senior year as one of the finest linebackers to attend Penn State. With great players, the Penn State Nittany Lions definitely earned their place in history!

1986 Record

Won	Lost	Fiesta Bowl
12	0	Beat University of Miami 14–10

Games played

Date	Vs	Result
Sept. 6	Temple	W, 45–15
Sept. 20	at Boston College	W, 26–14
Sept. 27	East Carolina	W, 42–17
Oct. 4	Rutgers	W, 31–6
Oct. 11	Cincinnati	W, 23–17
Oct. 18	Syracuse	W, 42–3
Oct. 25	at Alabama	W, 23–3
Nov. 1	at West Virginia	W, 19–0
Nov. 8	Maryland	W, 17–15
Nov. 15	at Notre Dame	W, 24–19
Nov. 22	Pittsburgh	W, 34–14

Fiesta Bowl, Tempe, Arizona

Jan. 2	Miami	W, 14–10

Miami quarterback Vinny Testaverde launches a pass in the 1987 Fiesta Bowl.

1995 University of Nebraska Cornhuskers

In 25 years at Nebraska, Tom Osborne never won fewer than 9 games in any season. But for 21 of those years, Osborne was worried he couldn't win a national title. In the 1984 Orange Bowl, after an 11–0 season, the Cornhuskers scored in the final moments to get within a point of Miami. Osborne chose to go for a **two-point conversion** instead of kicking the extra point and taking a tie. Nebraska failed to make the conversion, giving Miami the national title.

The 1995 Cornhuskers take the field in a game against Arizona State. The team won the game 77–28.

Brook Berringer (1973–1996)

Brook Berringer played quarterback on two Nebraska teams that won national championships, but he didn't live to see some of his teammates win a third. He died in a plane crash in April 1996 after graduating with a business degree in December. He got his chance to play when star Tommie Frazier was injured and proved he could run the Nebraska offense just as well. He had a strong arm and was a quick runner, and he was a leader his teammates respected. Today, Nebraska honors Berringer with an award and football scholarship in his memory that recognizes a football player's community service and hard work.

Osborne was a great coach and was elected into the College Football Hall of Fame in 1998. He was also named Coach of the Year in 1994. Osborne led Nebraska to national championships in 1994, 1995, and a co-championship in 1997. He also led the Cornhuskers to 25 straight bowl games! In his career he ended up with 255 wins, 49 losses, and 3 ties.

All-Americans
Tommie Frazier (QB)
Aaron Graham (T)
Jared Tomich (DT)

In 1994, Osborne finally won his title. Junior quarterback Tommie Frazier had started since his freshman year, but was found to have a blood clot behind his knee during the season. Junior Brook Berringer stepped in and went 7–0 as a starter to keep Nebraska in the running for a national title. With a powerful offensive line leading the way, Nebraska led the nation in rushing and beat Miami 24–17 in the Orange Bowl to cap off a 13–0 season.

The next season, Tommie Frazier was healthy again, and the Cornhuskers were unstoppable. Their offensive line was better than ever, clearing the way for running backs such as freshman Ahman Green. Nebraska's offensive line was made up of very big and fast players. They were able to beat their opponents to their spots. Behind Frazier, Green, and the other running backs, the Cornhuskers ran for over 400 yards a game, and in total averaged over 500 yards every game! Frazier couldn't be stopped, running and passing the ball all over the field. He was the most dangerous player in college football and very difficult to defend. Nebraska's defense was also big and strong. Jared Tomich was a force in the middle of the defense, throwing his body around and making tackles. Few teams could run the ball against the Huskers.

HISTORY BOX

No More Ties

For many years, a college football game that had a tie score when time ran out was over. There was no **overtime** to decide a winner. That cost Nebraska coach Tom Osborne a national title in 1983. At the end of the Orange Bowl, Nebraska scored a touchdown to get within a point of Miami. Osborne decided to attempt a two-point conversion to go for the win and insure a national championship, instead of kicking for one point and a tie. The Cornhuskers failed and lost the national championship. By the time Osborne won his second national title in 1995, college football was changing. Starting with the 1996 season, the NCAA introduced overtime and ties became a thing of the past.

The Cornhuskers extended their winning streak to 25 games in 1995 with another undefeated season and a national title. They averaged over 50 points per game. The Cornhuskers were one of the highest scoring and most dangerous offensive teams in the history of college football. Another impressive statistic from the 1995 season is that the Cornhuskers beat a total of 4 teams ranked in the top 10 that year and won those games by an average of 23 points.

Nebraska won each game that season by at least 14 points and defeated the University of Florida 62–24 in the Fiesta Bowl. With few weaknesses and so much power, sports expert Jeff Sagarin named the 1995 Nebraska team the best college football team of the second half of the 20th century. The entire team was so good that 27 players from that team eventually ended up playing in the NFL!

1995 Record

Won	Lost	Fiesta Bowl
12	0	Beat University of Florida 62–24

Games played

Date	Vs	Result
Aug. 31	at Oklahoma State	W, 64–21
Sept. 9	at Michigan State	W, 50–10
Sept. 16	Arizona State	W, 77–28
Sept. 23	Pacific	W, 49–7
Sept. 30	Washington State	W, 35–21
Oct. 14	Missouri	W, 57–0
Oct. 21	Kansas State	W, 49–25
Oct. 28	at Colorado	W, 44–21
Nov. 4	Iowa State	W, 73–14
Nov. 11	at Kansas	W, 41–3
Nov. 24	Oklahoma	W, 37–0

Fiesta Bowl, Tempe, Arizona

Jan. 2	Florida	W, 62–24

At the end of the season, Frazier finished second in voting for the Heisman Trophy. He still has the record for total offensive yardage gained at the University of Nebraska with 5,476 yards gained in his career. In his career as a starting quarterback at Nebraska, Frazier had an unbelievable 33 wins with only 3 losses.

Nebraska running back Ahman Green carries the football during the 1996 Fiesta Bowl.

1999 Florida State University Seminoles

From start to finish of the 1999 season, Florida State was the No. 1 team in the country. With receiver Peter Warrick catching the ball and 27-year-old quarterback Chris Weinke throwing it, the Seminoles were hard to stop. The two teamed up for one of the most exciting and unstoppable connections in college football. Weinke came to Florida State in 1997 after playing six years in minor-league baseball, making him college football's oldest quarterback. He went 32–3 as a starter and won the Heisman Trophy in 2000 as a senior. Warrick caught 71 passes and scored 12 touchdowns despite missing 2 games because of a suspension.

One of the greatest offensive teams of all time, Florida State's 1999 team gave coach Bobby Bowden his second national title in seven years. He added this to the national title they won in 1993. Bowden also picked up his 300th win that season. He did it by beating his son Tommy, the coach at Clemson, in the first ever college football father–son match up. The Seminoles put a big finish on the season by beating the No. 2 and No. 3 teams in the country in their final two games.

The 1999 Florida State Seminoles celebrate a win over Miami. It was their sixth straight win for the season.

Bobby Bowden (1929–)

Bobby Bowden has always had a personality that could be described as "grandfatherly." Who knew he'd still be coaching when he became an actual grandfather? Bowden came to Florida in 1976. He took over a team that had won only four games in the three seasons before he arrived and built it into a powerful team that won national titles. Florida State went to 26 bowl games in his 29 years at the school through 2005 and won national championships in 1993 and 1999. In 2003, he passed Joe Paterno in all-time wins. From 1985 to 1995, Florida State won eleven straight bowl games; an NCAA record. His sons Tommy and Terry both went on to become college football coaches.

Ranked number one in the **preseason**, the Seminoles had a tough early game with Georgia Tech University, who hung on until Florida State finally escaped with a 41–35 win. The Seminoles were 10–0 going into the last game of the regular season. The team was down 16-13 in the third quarter before they pulled away for a 30–23 win over Florida.

In the Sugar Bowl, they faced an undefeated Virginia Tech team led by an amazing freshman quarterback named Michael Vick. While Vick threw for one touchdown and ran for another, Florida State was just too good. Warrick caught 6 passes for 163 yards, including 2 touchdown passes for 64 and 43 yards, and returned a 59-yard punt for another touchdown. He also caught a pass for a two-point conversion, scoring a total of twenty points for Florida State. The Seminoles scored the game's final eighteen points to turn a one-point game in the third quarter into a blowout. Even at the end of the year, the Seminoles were too good to stop.

All-Americans

Peter Warrick (WR)
Sebastian Janikowski (K)
Corey Simon (DT)
Jason Whitaker (T)

Virginia Tech quarterback Michael Vick was a tough opponent for Florida State.

1999 Record

Won	Lost	Sugar Bowl
12	0	Beat Virginia Tech University 46–29

Games played

Date	Vs	Result
Aug. 28	Louisiana Tech	W, 41–7
Sept. 11	Georgia Tech	W, 41–35
Sept. 18	N.C. State	W, 42–11
Sept. 25	at North Carolina	W, 42–10
Oct. 2	Duke	W, 51–23
Oct. 9	Miami	W, 31–21
Oct. 16	Wake Forest	W, 33–10
Oct. 23	at Clemson	W, 17–14
Oct. 30	at Virginia	W, 35–10
Nov. 13	Maryland	W, 49–10
Nov. 20	at Florida	W, 30–23

Sugar Bowl, New Orleans

Jan. 4	Virginia Tech	W, 46–29

The Seminoles finished among the Associated Press' top four teams in the country in 1999 for the thirteenth straight year. It was also the thirteenth straight year of winning ten games or more in one season. This team had many great individual players, and at the end of the year, when the awards were given out, it showed. The kicker, Sebastian Janikowski, was named the nation's best kicker for the second year in a row. Florida State also led the nation in the number of players chosen to the Associated Press' All-American first team, with four players—Janikowski, Warrick, defensive tackle Corey Simon, and tackle Jason Whitaker. Warrick also finished in sixth place for the Heisman Trophy.

HISTORY BOX

Speed Rules

For decades, how many games a team won had a lot to do with the size of the team's players. Big linemen blocked for big running backs, while big defensive linemen and linebackers tried to stop them. Two schools in Florida thought they saw a better way. Howard Schnellenberger at Miami and Bobby Bowden at Florida State didn't have a whole lot of big players to recruit in Florida, but there were plenty of fast ones. They liked to put fast players on the field and make a few big plays instead of a lot of little ones. Miami's upset of Nebraska in the Orange Bowl to win the 1983 national title was the first of seven national titles for Miami, Florida, and Florida State over the next eighteen years. With their speed, they dominated the college game.

The Final Score

It is almost impossible to narrow college football's great teams down to just ten. So many great teams and great players have been left out. But that is part of the fun of college football, because there have been so many greats.

The University of Miami and Ohio State University aren't on this list, although they are two of college football's great schools. In the 2003 Fiesta Bowl, they played for the national title. After Miami appeared to have the game won in the fourth quarter, Ohio State won in overtime. Both teams were full of talented players who went on to play in the NFL. Both teams' success is remembered to this day.

Many of today's great college football programs, such as Notre Dame, have roots that extend back early into the 20th century. Some traditional powers, such as Army, have found it hard to keep up as the game has become so popular. Still, the great Army teams of the past are still remembered as the champions they were in their day.

One of the great things about college football is that it extends across the country. There are exciting teams to be found on both coasts, in the Midwest, and in the South. Just about everywhere, there's been a great team or there is a great team now. There are many rivalries that fans look forward to during the college football season, such as the University of Michigan versus Ohio State University, the University of Florida versus Florida State University, and the University of Notre Dame versus the University of Southern California. Fans have fun watching these intense games, and players feed off of this excitement.

A new argument begins every fall. Is this year's national champion one of the ten best of all time? That debate lasts for almost a year until the new season begins. Each year, fans watch to see if this will be the season a new champion is added to the list of true greats.

Timeline

1869: Princeton University plays Rutgers University in the first acknowledged college football game.

1925: 1924 University of Notre Dame Fighting Irish defeat Stanford University in the Rose Bowl 27–10.

1926: The Army–Navy game becomes the first to draw 100,000 spectators.

1935: Jay Berwanger becomes the first player to win the Heisman Trophy.

1936: For the first time, a poll of sportswriters is used to determine the national champion.

1962: 1961 University of Alabama Crimson Tide defeat Arkansas in the Sugar Bowl 10–3.

1972: 1971 University of Nebraska Cornhuskers defeat Alabama in the Orange Bowl 38–6.

1973: 1972 University of Southern California Trojans defeat Ohio State University in the Rose Bowl 42–17.

1987: 1986 Pennsylvania State University Nittany Lions defeat Miami in the Fiesta Bowl 14–10.

1996: 1995 University of Nebraska Cornhuskers defeat Florida in the Fiesta Bowl 62–24.

1996: The NCAA introduces overtime to decide tied games.

2000: 1999 Florida State University Seminoles defeat Virginia Tech in the Sugar Bowl 46–29.

2003: Ohio State University defeats Miami in the Fiesta Bowl 31–24. This is the first time a national title is decided in overtime.

2004: University of Southern California Trojans defeat Oklahoma in the Orange Bowl 55–19.

Glossary

All-American college football writers' honor for the season's best player at each position

backfield skill players who are positioned behind the offensive line. This includes the quarterback and running backs.

Bowl Championship Series attempt by the NCAA to match the top two teams each season in a national championship game

bowl game extra game awarded to teams who finish the season with a winning record

conference group of schools together, such as the Big ten conference

debate argument

dominant leader. A dominant team is one that seems unbeatable.

extra point after scoring a touchdown, a team has the option to kick the ball through the goal posts for one point

field goal kicking the ball through the goalpost to gain three points

fullback often the ball-carrier in the early days of football, today most fullbacks are big blockers and inside runners

halfback also known as a "tailback," the running back who most often carries the football

Heisman Trophy award presented annually by New York's Downtown Athletic Club to the best college player

huddle players grouped together, usually in a circle, to call plays

inspire motivate people to do well

interception when a defensive player catches a pass intended for an offensive player

lineman defensive or offensive player positioned directly on the line of scrimmage

linebacker defenders positioned directly behind the defensive lineman

National Collegiate Athletic Association (NCAA) association of colleges and universities in the United States who set standards and rules for student athletes

National Football League (NFL) major professional football league in the United States

overtime extra playing periods added to the game when it ends in a tie

polls collection of votes

preseason period before the college football season begins

promote try to make something more popular

punter player that turns the ball over to the opponents with a kick

quarter one of four parts to a football game. Each quarter is 15 minutes.

quarterback player who takes the snap from the center and runs the offense

running back player that is positioned behind the quarterback and runs or rushes the football

shut out when a team stops its opponent from scoring any points

sneak when the quarterback runs right behind the center once he receives the snap

Super Bowl championship game of the NFL

tight end sixth offensive lineman who is also a pass receiver

touchdown run or pass that crosses the goal line into the end zone

two-point conversion after scoring a touchdown, a team has the option to run or throw the ball into the end zone for two points

Further Information

Further reading

Buckley, Jr., James. *Football*. New York:
Dorling Kindersley Publishing Inc., 2000

Griffin, Gwen. *Irish Legends: The Notre Dame Fighting Irish Story*.
Mankato, MN: The Creative Company, 1999

Owens, Thomas S. *Football Stadiums*. Minneapolis:
Twenty-First Century Books, Inc., 2004

Addresses

College Football Hall of Fame
111 South Street
South Bend, IN 46601

Paul W. Bryant Museum
University of Alabama
300 Bryant Drive
Tuscaloosa, AL 35487
www.bryantmuseum.ua.edu

Pro Football Hall of Fame
2121 George Halas Drive NW
Canton, Ohio 44708
www.profootballhof.com

National Collegiate Athletic Association (NCAA)
www2.ncaa.org

Index